# CELCIC DESIGN

**Aidan Meehan** studied Celtic art in Ireland and Scotland
and has spent the last two decades playing a leading role
in the renaissance of this authentic tradition. He has given
workshops, demonstrations and lectures in Europe and the
USA, and more recently throughout the Pacific North West
from his home base in Vancouver, B.C., Canada.

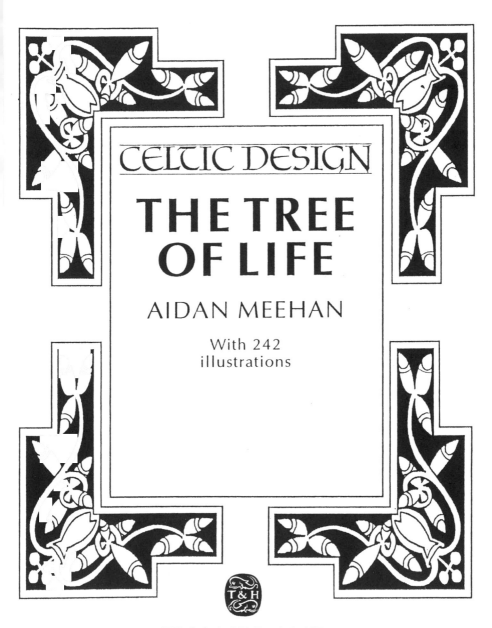

# CELTIC DESIGN

# THE TREE OF LIFE

### AIDAN MEEHAN

With 242
illustrations

THAMES AND
HUDSON

This Book is Dedicated to
my daughter Hannah Joy
and to Dianne Bjornson,
Forest Dweller Extraordinaire

artwork and calligraphy
copyright © 1995 Aidan Meehan

First published in the United States of America in 1995
by Thames and Hudson Inc., 500 Fifth Avenue,
New York, New York 10110

Library of Congress Catalog Card Number 94-61399

ISBN 0-500-27827-X

Printed and bound in Great Britain

[ 5 ]

# ᴛHE ÇOLᴆEN BOUÇH

*Blessed is the man who has found wisdom...*
*Her ways are good ways,*
*and all her paths are peaceful,*
*She is a tree of life to all that lay hold upon her*
— PROVERBS 3:18

 HE TREE OF LIFE is an ancient motif, symbolising life's unity. In Celtic art it appears in the mid–eighth–century, as in the Book of Kells, where it typically stems from a little chalice, *fig. la.* It must have been introduced about then, as it is not in the Book of Lindisfarne of AD 698. But although the tree in the illuminated gospels is a Christian symbol, naturally, this is not its only meaning, nor even its origin.

[ 7 ]

Fig. 1    Tree of Life, The Book of Kells,
          Detail

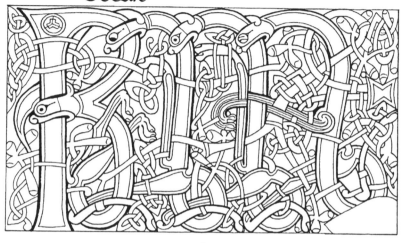

a

b

Fig. 2    The Tree, extracted

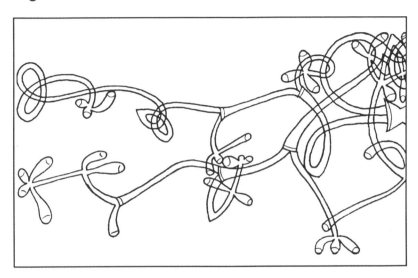

Fig. 1a is taken from a detail of a page in the Book of Kells. It is the Tree of Life inhabited by four lions, spelling out the letters RIN, *fig. 1b*. The plan of the tree is extracted here in draft form, *fig. 2*. The tree is seen weaving sideways through the warp of letters, filling their voids and interspaces willy-nilly. Taken out of context like this, it looks lop-sided. It is usually more symmetrical.

Fig. 3    The same, detail

Still, it points up the definition of the Celtic Tree of Life given by George Bain when he coined the name for the motif: "It will be observed that in every example, the tree or plant has a logical

 growth. It branches from the main stem to form cornucopiae from which other branches with leaves emerge. These have more resemblance to mistletoe than to any other plant. "

The Celtic Tree of Life cannot truly be identified as any one species, no more than the lion-dogs or eagle-cranes of Celtic animal patterns. But out of all that I have seen, this extracted tree resembles mistletoe the most. It has had to seek out room between the letters, like the light-hungry sprig in the branches of an oak.

Whether the Celtic Tree of Life *is*
mistletoe or not, it certainly is not a
grapevine, as has been suggested. I think
of it as a Celtic version of Frazer's Golden
Bough. Virgil describes this magical
branch, and compares it to mistletoe on
an oak. The Latin poet tells how Aeneas,
in his quest for the Golden Bough, saw
two birds alight upon a tree, "whence
shone a flickering gleam of gold. As in
the woods in winter cold the mistletoe
– a plant not native to its tree – is green
with fresh leaves and twines its yellow
berries about the boles; such seemed
upon the shady oak the leafy gold, so
rustled in the gentle breeze the golden
leaf." But how can the mistletoe be
called the Golden Bough? It is green with
white berries, not yellow. Frazer suggests
that "Golden Bough" may well have been an
old Celtic name for mistletoe, as it is called
"the tree of pure gold" in Welsh. Perhaps
some Celtic bard read Virgil, or *vice versa*!

In Frazer's view also, mistletoe was called golden because gold is the sun's colour. It was thought to be the very life of the oak tree, and the seed of the sun. It was seen as the life of the oak because it grows green on the leafless tree, and as solar seed because the flame released from the yule log was thought to revive the midwinter sun.

Mistletoe grows on the oak, not on the ground. This links it symbolically to heaven rather than earth, and makes it a symbol of the spirit dwelling in the body but not of it, as the mistletoe in the oak is suspended between earth and heaven. In his *Dictionary of Symbols*, Tom Chetwynd defines gold as "the enduring and untarnishable essence of life, whatever is of the highest value." Mistletoe is certainly a symbol of the enduring essence of the oak: the plant that reveals life's persistence in the leafless tree also indicates what is of most value, survival. So gold

symbolises the immortality of the spirit,
the spark that glows within the mortal
soul, just as the green mistletoe on the
naked branch points to the perennial
hope of survival through and beyond the
grave of winter.

In many legends, the object of the
quest is a golden object, often hung upon
a magic tree – the Golden Apples of the
Sun, the Golden Fleece. The tree refers to
the life of the cosmos, its very source
rooted in the ground of being, and its
fruit, the treasure which many set out to
find but few obtain, fully-realised
identity. The Cosmic Tree is a universal
idea, and a very ancient one, as relevant
today as ever. The view of the Tree as
sacred goes back to when we lived among
the trees, or even *in* them.

Trevelyan describes it vividly. "For
many centuries after Britain became an
island the untamed forest was king. Its
moist and mossy floor was hidden from

heaven's eye by a close-drawn curtain
woven of innumerable tree-tops, which
shivered in the breezes of summer dawn
and broke into wild music of millions
upon millions of birds; the concert was
prolonged from bough to bough with
scarcely a break for hundreds of miles
over hill and plain and mountain,
unheard by man save where, at rarest
intervals, a troop of skin-clad hunters,
stone axe in hand, moved furtively over
the ground beneath, ignorant that they
lived upon an island, not dreaming that
there could be other parts of the world
besides this damp, green woodland with
its meres and marshes, wherein they
hunted, a terror to its four-footed
inhabitants and themselves afraid. "

I can follow the picture Trevelyan
paints up to the terror at the end, where
man comes in. The fear he projects was
hardly shared by the stone-age hunters.
The forest dwellers' normal state of mind

## Fig. 4      Three Animal Letters

These three letters are from fig. 1b, above, where they are extricated and separated from the background in order to isolate the tree. Taken thus out of context, the knotwork is not as organised as it would be if the letters were on their own. There is no point copying them as they are there, for they are missing all the points of interlacement with the tree, together with which they make completely satisfactory knots. A little bit of licence is called for, so here they are, tidied up. Like the Tree of Life, they have a logic of their own, with manes drawn out into top knots, and tails forming the background filler. The knots are the thinnest, and the bodies are the widest bands, with the limbs of a middling thickness. The use of three widths gives the pattern a harmonious variety. I have drawn more animal letters from the Book of Kells in a previous book in the Celtic Design series, Illuminated Letters, where you can find an entire alphabet of lions, to which these clearly belong.

was more likely to be in tune with that
of the Amazonian Indian: "the trees are
Earth's bones, earth is flesh and rivers and
streams are veins: when we cut down all
the trees, we kill our own selves". Trees
literally meant the world, indeed life
itself, to those first inhabitants of Britain
described by Trevelyan.

By 4,000 years ago, before the earliest
Indo-Europeans moved west and south-
east, giant oak forests blanketed Europe.
The oak tree came to symbolise life because it provided a bountiful supply of
food and fuel and lumber, the memory of
which gave rise to our myths of origin in
the garden. So many creation myths re-
call a golden age, a Paradise, but if there
was an Eden then, it had no walls. We
never fell from it, we felled it.

For many thousands of years longer
than have ever been recorded, living with
the murmur of oak leaves in our ears, the
constant, majestic presence of the forest

entered deep into us, there to be distilled
into a psychic model of the universe, the
World Tree. The oak became the icon of
the world to those for whom the forest
was the world.

Just how deeply the archetypal oak
affected us may be fathomed from its long-
lost name: " In fact, our words 'truth',
'trust', and 'tree' can all be traced back
four thousand years to an ancient Proto-
Indo-European word for oak. They called
it *dorw*, which also meant 'firm', 'strong',
'enduring'. . . ," as James Powell tells us
in *The Tao of Symbols*.

Powell goes on to tell how, when they
moved into India, the Proto-Indo-Europeans
left behind the oak tree of their home-
lands, but took it with them everywhere
they went, in their language. The Sanscrit
word for tree is *daru*, which is related to
the ancient word for oak. So too is the
Sanscrit word for the Pole Star, *dhruva*,
"the abiding, the firm or fixed one".

Fig. 5    Tree of Life Motif, Book of Kells

e

5a The pencilled centre-line sketch.

5b The outline follows the centre line.

5c The woven tree, pencilled over the outline.

5d The inked design with background filled in.

5e This motif makes a useful corner decoration.

---

What has the Pole Star got to do with oak trees? Well, the pole in question is none other than the "axletree", and, to a tribe of cattle-driving charioteers, perhaps the world *had* become a wheel that turned upon a spindle. I think that the words for oak and axle were once the same because the essence of an axle is to stay firmly fixed, and last a long time. The same principle applies to a tree.

*Dorw* meant more than just a certain brand of tree, but, rather, its adamantine qualities: as an aged oak embodies fixity, hardness, longevity beyond record, so too the Pole Star, *dhruva*, was revered as a shining embodiment of three attributes of *dorw*: the Abiding, the Firm, the Fixed.

The same qualities of oak also survive in several English D-R words such as durable (stable, constant, continuing, firm, persistent); endure (long lasting); duress (hardship) and duration (continuance over time). These all derive from Latin, *durare*,

to last, and *durus*, hard. Both these words
neatly hold on to the same oak qualities we
met with in the Proto-Indo-European *dorw*.

This D-R sound survives in other
Indo-European words linked to oak as
referring to fixity in space or time. In
Greek there is *drus*, oak; *drimus*, hard;
*diorthono*, fixed. The sense of time is
also felt in Greek *diarkes*, durable, per-
manent; *diarkeia*, duration; *diarreo*,
elapse. The Gaelic word for oak is *dair*,
while *doire*, oak grove, gave us Irish
place-names such as Derry, Durrow,
and Kildare. The Firm turns up in *daoire*,
hardness, while Abiding is implied in
*deireanach*, last or late, and *deireadh*, end
(as of a period of time).

*Druid* is likewise related to *dorw*.
Gaulish *druida* and Irish *draoi*, Druid,
are said to be derived from *druwids*,
wise man of the oaks, whence *draiodoir*,
a wizard, also.

However, it seems safe to say that the

Druids derived their name from *some* D-R root. No wonder, then, the epithet they favoured among themselves was, "the Strong". It does take a certain strength of mind to remain fixed firmly on the abiding things of life.

Finally, it hardly matters if the Tree of Life in Celtic art is mistletoe or vine. The Tree is, simply, all that lasts, stays true – and remains put – throughout all the fragility, fickleness, and transience of happenstance.

# THE WINGED LION

*The glories of Mary held his soul captive
... her emblems, the lateflowering plant
and lateblossoming tree - James Joyce*

ND THE LORD GOD SAID, Behold, the man is become as one of us, to know good and evil: and now, lest he put forth his hand, and take also of the tree of life, and eat, and live for ever: therefore the Lord God sent him forth from the garden of Eden to till the ground from whence he was taken. So he drove out the man; and he placed at the east of the garden of Eden Cherubims, and a flaming sword which turned every way, to keep the way of the tree of life (Genesis 3: 22–24).

Fig. 6    Winged Lion and Lopped Tree,
          North Cross, Dulleek, Ireland

 On the North Cross at Dulleek there is a little carved panel of a winged lion holding what looks like a broom, but is in fact a pole mounted on a pyramidal base, like the shaft of a Celtic cross.  The creature is related to a pair of very similar winged lions holding a palm, on a carved stone cross at Durrow Abbey, *fig. 7*.  Henry Crawford says of the palm tree between two winged lions: "this is an interesting example of one of the oldest and most widely spread of symbolic designs, but it is difficult to say how it came to be on an Irish Christian monument.  It is found on Assyrian slabs and cylinders, and on certain ancient buildings in Asia Minor."

Fig. 7    Palm Tree between Lions,
Durrow Abbey, Ireland

The fact that both the pole and the
palm tree are represented with the same
creature – a winged lion – on crosses at
Durrow and Dulleek points up the symbolic equivalence between the tree and
pillar. The pillar is, after all, actually a
lopped tree trunk. Crawford adds that
variations of the design have men wor-
shipping instead of animals, and a pillar
or altar instead of the palm tree. The
pyramidal base may have been intended to
suggest an altar, as it certainly does
when supporting a Celtic cross shaft.
Tree and pillar are also related in that
both have been used as symbols of the

World Axis, symbolising the central principle of the universe. Consequently, both tree and pillar have been used as substitutes for that ultimate symbol of the sacred centre, the cross.

A cross may be seen as a simplified diagram of the Tree of Life: the vertical axis representing the trunk and the horizontal axis the branches. The union of heaven and earth as symbolised by the tree or pillar is also symbolised by the cross, the horizontal line referring to the terrestrial plane, the vertical to the celestial axis. Corresponding to the shaft of the cross, the Cosmic Pillar is likewise an emblem of divine incarnation, penetrating the human plane from above and supporting it from below, as the shaft of the cross intersects the horizontal arm. Thus the Tree of Life, the Cosmic Pillar or the cross may be exchanged for one another, chiefly because they refer to the same idea, that of a central, divine principle.

Fig. 8        Greek Carving, Priene

Pillar and tree unite in this figure,
with griffins in place of lions. A griffin
is both eagle and lion and as seen in *The
Dragon and the Griffin*, it is the prototype
of the German-style animal that entered
Celtic art first in the seventh-century Book
of Durrow, and again after the Vikings.
It is a royal crest, combining animals of
earth and sky, and so relates to the cross
as a symbol of the union of heaven and
earth, which is how the griffin came to
be an emblem of Christ in medieval art.

## Fig. 9    Tetramorph, Trier Gospel

The man holds a sword in his left hand, and in his sword hand a flowering rod, offering peace before sharp judgement. A leather cloak slung over his left shoulder is girt with eagle wings and claws, hindlegs of a lion and of a calf. The order of the symbols, calf, lion, eagle and man reflect the four seasons, as well as the four Ages of Man. His grey hair and beard, hollow cheeks and lined face identify him as being in the winter of his years. Both his feet are turned to the left, in the Irish style of the Book of Durrow: here he not only walks like an Egyptian hieroglyph, but holds his sword and flower like the crook and flail of Osiris.

An Assyrian-style winged lion might well have been included on a Medieval Irish cross as the winged lion is the emblem of St Mark. The symbols of the four evangelists ultimately derive from Mesopotamian astrology. The evangelist symbols of Homo, Vitulus, Leo and Aquila correspond to the zodiacal symbols for Aquarius, Taurus, Leo and Scorpio (the Eagle is the regenerate aspect of Scorpio).

These signs corresponding to the four quarters of the year describe the Cross of the Heavens. The early monks found the sign of the cross imprinted on the fabric of time as well as space as the four fixed signs of the zodiac. The creatures were sometimes represented with four wings, and refer to the visions of Ezekiel and St John, four wings signifying cherubim in the angelic hierarchy. Their attributes are found combined in the Tetramorph of the Trier Gospel, *fig.9*. The Calf, the Lion, and the Eagle form the man's apron.

## Fig. 10   Figure between Two Lions, Cretan Gem

I find it more difficult to account for the appearance of a minotaur on the Market Cross at Kells, *fig. 11*. It derives from a variant of the winged lions and tree motif which has been called "the Daemon between Two Lions" and also "the Lord of the Beasts", where a figure replaces the pillar or tree, *fig. 10*. The Market Cross figure has a lion's tail, and grasps the tails of his familiars, who whisper in his ear. The figure between two beasts was originally a sun symbol, the animals gnawing at him from either side causing the days to shorten, whereas the solar victor was often depicted holding two beasts at bay, or trampling them. The figure on the Cretan gem appears to have

Fig. 11   Trimorph between Two Lions,
          Market Cross, Kells

tamed his attendant lions, patting their
heads, indicating the equinox or balance
between forces of light and dark.

Another variant of this motif is the
triumph of the two lions devouring the
sun right down to a complete standstill,
the solstice point, with
just a head between
their gaping maws, as
on the Pictish cross-
slab at Dunfallandy,
*fig.* 13. Here the beast is
a sea serpent with per-
haps a wolf's head in
place of a lion's.  The
back of the Pictish cross-slab from which
this figure has been drawn, and which
has been described as "a page in stone",
may well be compared with several
pages of the Book of Kells framed with
lion-headed, fish-tailed serpents.

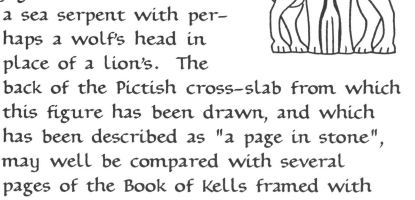

Fig. 12   Christ with Two Lion-Dragons,
         Book of Kells, folio 2v, AD 750

Both variants of the solstice motif
occur in Celtic and Germanic art from
way back, and later in the Book of Kells,
where the white-robed figure of Christ
is shown between the heads of two lion-
dragons, grasping their tongues, *fig. 12*.
The figure twisting the lions by their
tails on the Market Cross at Kells, *fig. 11*,
seems to be on more familiar terms with
his lions. It has been suggested that he
is the old Celtic horned god, Cernunnos,

Fig. 13   Head Between two Monsters,
Pictland, AD 750

the Lord of the Stags in Gaul, but the
stag god should have antlers, not horns.
A likelier candidate might be the Irish
sun god, Bile, who is related to the god
Baal, or Biblical Golden Calf, which might
at least be thought to account for his
horns.

However, the character on the Kells
Cross is most likely a compound of three
evangelist symbols, with the horns of the
Calf, the tail of the Lion, and the body of
the Man. I think this is so, especially as
it is located in the Market Place at Kells,
where the Book of Kells used to be, and

could be consulted. On the page of the
Book of Kells where a figure holds two
lions' tongues, *fig.* 12, he rises from behind an arched vault containing a man, a
lion and a calf-headed eagle. On Folio 3r
he appears behind or out of a golden tree
with two birds on it (shades of Virgil's
Golden Bough), between two lions, above
an arch containing only three evangelist
symbols, man, lion and calf; overleaf,
folio 3v, is a calf-lion combination. On
the next page however, folio 4r, the man
and the eagle gaze at a frontal view of a
calf-lion, which may have inspired the
Market Cross design. If two of the four
evangelist symbols can be merged like
this in the Book of Kells, why not three –
the man, the lion and the calf – on the
Cross of Kells?

In the Book of Kells, f. 2v ( *fig.* 12 ) ,
incidentally, the tails of the lion-serpents
are hidden in the vase-shaped capital of a
pillar supporting the arch of a vault

surmounted by the white-clad, solar form of Christ. The capitals support the vault as the Cosmic Pillar supports the sky. Intriguingly, the lion-headed snake comes out of the beaker on top of the cauldron in the same way that the Tree of Life grows out of its pot. The column looks more like an inkwell on a stand than a classical column, perhaps intentionally. The lower part of the capital is cauldron shaped, so the whole column is more likely intended to suggest the shape of a tall, eucharistic chalice. Behind four such columns float three circular frames resting on stands, each with a central roundel, suggesting the form of a liturgical vessel used for displaying the consecrated host on an altar. Columns and roundels, then, may be taken to refer to the communion bread and wine.

In the Welsh Book of St Chad, *fig. 14*, St Luke is shown with two insignia, a gold cross with a rosy, eight-petalled flower, and a staff branching into two spirals, each with seven little shamrock leaves pointed like candle flames. These represent two different sorts of Tree of Life, the Rose Cross and the Miraculous Sprouting Staff. St Luke is framed by a white-stippled sea serpent with two dogs' heads facing away from, not towards him. Here St Luke replaces the Solar Hero. The canine heads of the double serpent may be compared to the two wolf-like heads of the Pictish cross-slab of Dunfallandy, *fig. 13*, carved shortly after the time of the Book of Kells. The eight-petalled rosette is also a symbol of the sacred centre, used in place of the cross in early Celtic Christianity. Here it is combined with the ring of the Celtic cross. It corresponds, then, to the eight-petalled flower of the Trier Tetramorph, *fig. 9*, where The Man holds a rod and sword also crossed over like the emblems of St Luke in the Book of Chad. Françoise Henry calls this

Fig. 14   Portrait of St Luke,
          Gospels of St Chad, Wales

Fig. 15   Archangel with Flowering Rod,
          Book of Kells

crossing of the insignia of
spiritual authority "the
Osiris Pose".

Osiris, who dies and is
revived, the judge of the
dead, holds the flail and
shepherd's crook with his
arms crossed. There is also
a mythical association between Osiris and the Tree
of life. After he was killed,
Osiris' coffin was thrown
into the Nile. It drifted to
a far-off shore, where a magnificent tree
grew up, enclosing it. The tree then
came to the attention of a local king,
who had it cut down and made into the
pillar for his palace. Isis, wandering in
search of Osiris' body, came by this
pillar, which burst into leaf upon her
passing footfall whereby she recovered

Fig. 16    Illuminated Letter M,
           Book of Kells, folio 12r

The figure behind the letter is holding a branching
and a flowering rod. The shafts of the rods echo the
form of the pot of the Celtic Tree of Life and of
the gourd, both symbols of the womb.

# Fig. 17  Flowering Rods, Book of Kells

a

b

c

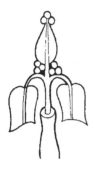

d

the burden of her quest. The flowering
Djed pillar thus became an emblem of
resurrection in Egypt. In Celtic art its
equivalent is the flowering rod, or the
branching sceptre, humbler versions of
the Tree of Life. Held diagonally cross-
wise, the rods form the letter X, the
Cross of Resurrection.

In truncated form, as Midsummer
Night itself is shortened, the two-headed
sea serpent recurs in the Durham
Cassiodorus, *fig. 18*. David here holds
both a lance and a ring divided by his
own name. The inscribed circle refers to
the royal house of David, from which
Christ's genealogy is traced. David's fa-
ther was Jesse, so that Christ is said to
be sprung from "Jesse's Tree" - another
possible reference of the Tree of Life.

As much a mate to the Grail Cup as
to his royal coronet, the lance links earth
to heaven diagonally through David's
own thus transfixed heart.

## Fig. 18 David, Durham Cassiodorus

### (Note leaf-shaped spearhead.)

# THE SERPENT ON THE TREE

*He shall be like a tree planted by the rivers of water,*
*that bringeth forth his fruit in his season;*
*his leaf also shall not wither;*
*and whatsoever he doeth shall prosper – Psalm 1,3*

THE GARDEN OF EDEN is obviously associated with the Tree of Life, and there we meet the snake on the other tree in Paradise, the Tree of Knowledge of Good and Evil, or duality. The serpent is usually portrayed on Celtic crosses in representations of the Biblical Fall, but almost never portrayed on the Celtic Tree of Life, which is usually filled with birds or cats.

[ 43 ]

The symbolism of the serpent on the tree is intimately linked to that of the winged lions guarding the Tree of Life. For example, there is the famous image carved on the green steatite vase of King Gudea of Lagash, inscribed about 2025 BC, *fig. 19*. It is dedicated to the serpent god Ningizzida, "Lord of the Tree of Truth", and consort of the goddess. Joseph Campbell describes the image as two copulating vipers entwined along a staff, flanked by "two winged dragons of a type known as the lion-bird". He compares the snakes to the caduceus of Hermes, the emblem of the medical profession. But on closer inspection, the two are actually one, with two heads. The serpent has two aspects, and combines opposites of masculine and feminine in itself, as expressed in its motion, from one side to another, on both land and water, and in the shape of its head, which changes from a male to a female symbol when its jaws gape, *fig. 21*.

Fig. 19    The Serpent Lord, Sumerian Vase

## Fig. 20    The Serpent on the Tree

From a painted Elamite bowl of the Late Sassanian Period (AD 226-641). The date palm tree closely resembles a branching pillar. On opposite sides are two fruits, corresponding to the sun and the moon, with the serpent inclining towards the lunar fruit.

## Fig. 21 The Head of the Serpent

a   b   c   d

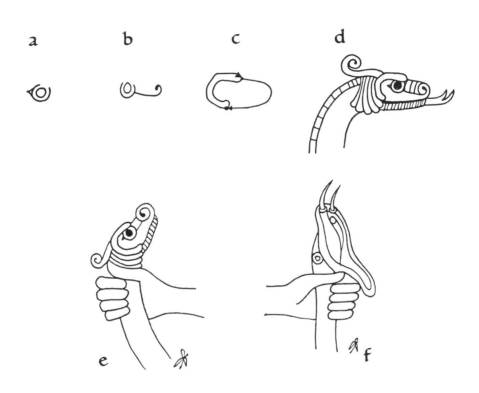

e   f

"The phallic suggestion is immediate, and, as swallower, the female organ is also suggested; so that a dual image is rendered, which works implicitly on the sentiments."   – Joseph Campbell

Fig. 22  Two-headed Serpent, Late Sumer

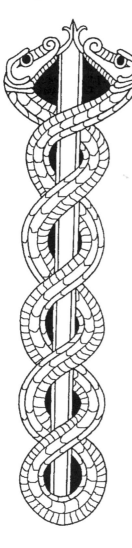

The double-headed serpent of Gudea's vase, then, *fig. 22*, symbolises the union of opposites around the central, synthesing principle, which also is the meaning of the sun and the moon flanking the tree on the painted Elamite vase, *fig. 20*. A form of the symbol appears on a carved panel surmounted by the Hand of God, *fig. 23*, on the Cross of Muiredach, Monasterboice Abbey, Ireland. The same cross has a depiction of Christ in Judgement with a cross and a branching rod, like that of St Luke in the Gospel of St Chad, *fig. 14*.

Fig. 23  Hand of God, Muiredach's Cross,
Monasterboice Abbey

The haloed right hand proffers the round communion
wafer. It is carved under the ring of the cross,
where the viewer has to look up to see, whereupon
the image is that of the hand about to place the
host on the tongue of the communicant. The right
hand is shown reversed for this reason. The
opposite side of the cross has the heads and serpents
repeated, but with two lions instead of the hand.
At the bottom of the same cross are two cats.

[ 49 ]

# Fig. 24   Twined Serpents, from an Early Akkadian Seal, c. 2200 BC

In the words of Joseph Campbell, this mystery cult scene shows "the deity in human form, enthroned, with his caduceus emblem behind and a fire altar before". He offers a horn of the elixir of immortality, indicated by the crescent moon which symbolises the cyclical renewal of life through death, as the new moon grows out of the old. Before him burns the purging fire, with three flames. Approaching the altar of purification is the spirit of the mortal entering the afterlife, led by the hand by a crowned male divinity, and attended by a female figure crowned with the serpent symbol of rebirth, carrying a pail. On either side are a pair of copulating snakes, twisting around an invisible vertical axis.

Yet another panel on Muiredach's Cross shows the Tree of Life inhabited by lions with two birds on top, as illustrated at the Frontispiece. The twined serpents are opposed, one pointing up and one pointing down. They enclose three heads, which, taken with the Hand of God above might be interpreted as representing the Holy Trinity. The helix of twisted snakes is found on an early Akkadian Seal, from about 2200 BC, where they form columns flanking the cult scene shown in *fig. 24*.

The symbol of the tree or pillar is replaced by the serpent helix between two figures of Gilgamesh on a Syro-Hittite seal, *fig. 25*. Twelve coils are shown along the axis of the column, corresponding to the zodiac. The thirteenth is hidden by the attendants' hands, perhaps signifying the central point around which the twelve turn. A symbol of the Sun, or the Pole Star, surmounts the *Axis Mundi*, like the star on a Christmas Tree.

# Fig. 25   Cosmic Pillar, Syro-Hittite Seal

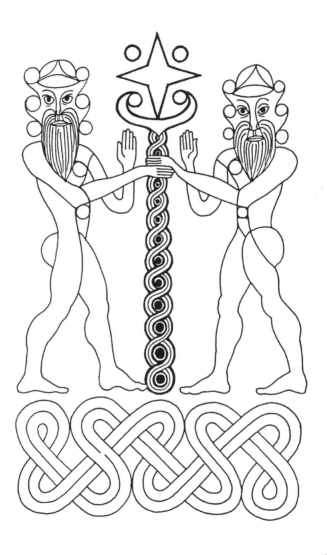

# TWO BIRDS ON ONE TREE

*Two birds, fast bound companions,*
*clasp close the self-same tree.*

—Mundaka Upanishad

R. A. K. COOMARASWAMY, the long-time Curator of the Museum of Fine Arts, Boston, and untiring champion of the traditional as sacred art, encouraged George Bain's conviction, arrived at towards the end of his career, that Celtic art belongs to a mainstream pervading all the sacred arts of the world.

In the preface to his seminal book, *Celtic Art, the Methods of Construction,* Bain appends a letter, dated June 1947, concerning the two birds on the Tree of Life,

Fig. 26  Two Birds on One Tree,
        Book of Kells, folio 129v, Layout

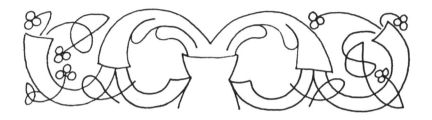

*Variation I: pencil layout of tree*

in which Coomaraswamy affirms that
they are a symbol of friendship between
the spirit and the soul – the *two* birds
on a tree represent the universal and
individualised selves (true self and Ego).

According to one tradition, one bird
selfishly eats the fruit while the other
looks on. One is the experiencer that takes
things personally and the other the witness, that core identity shared by all.

Fig. 27   Two Birds on One Tree,
Book of Kells, folio 129v, Layout

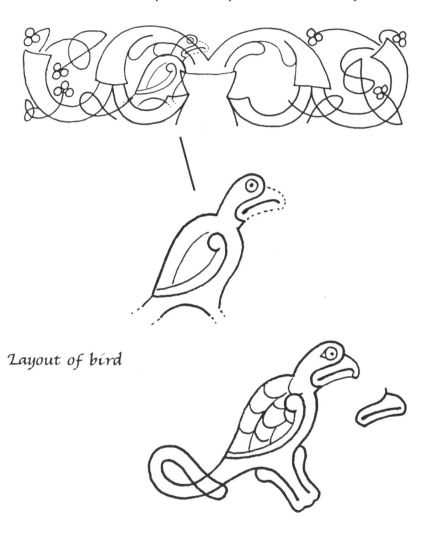

Layout of bird

# Fig. 28  Two Birds on One Tree, Book of Kells, 129v, variation

Variation I

Tree plus two birds. Notice different knots at either end, and triquetra knot at lower right corner.

The stem of the tree is split, or lobed, in the first section, passing over and under the beak. The knot at the upper right has a lobe at the sharp turn.

It is important to understand that when dealing with universal symbols such as the Tree of Life, we are dealing with a language of archetypal forms, like dreams, which arise spontaneously at all times and transmit themselves between all cultures. This is why analogies and connections may be drawn between medieval and ancient neolithic sources, in dealing with the content of art, as opposed to the datum of art history. It may be tempting, as Françoise Henry pointed out, to suggest a connection between Coptic and Celtic Christianity as the explanation for the "Osiris pose" in Celtic art, but no Coptic intermediary links have been found, as yet, that would validate such a suggestion from the historian's point of view, and so it remains a speculation.

But in dealing with the images as intelligible symbols, rather than just as anthropological data, the artist is not, as

### Fig. 29   Two Birds on One Tree, Book of Kells, folio 129v

Variation 2

Here the stem is lobed, and sprouts a trefoil filler before the first trumpet mouth. The beaks cross the whole stem of the tree.

The three-quarter turn spiral ends in a large, loosely defined palmette of four or five lobes.

# Fig. 30 Two Birds on One Tree, Book of Kells, folio 129v

Variation 3

The quarter-turn spiral branch is looped around itself in a basic knot, ending in a trefoil, left, and a cinquefoil, right.

The lobed stem splits at the base and weaves through the beak. The lobes are capped with ovoids.

# Fig. 31    Two Birds on One Tree, Book of Kells, folio 129v

Variation 4

Here the knots at either end have lobes at the sharp turn, and there are triquetras filling the lower corners.

The spiral branch around the bird ends in three dots. The feet of the bird are small, toe and thumb are not woven.

Coomaraswamy says: "reading into these intelligible forms an arbitrary meaning, but simply reading their meaning, for this is their form or life, and in them present, regardless of whether the individual artists of a given period, or we, have known it or not. "

In the twentieth century a great ferment has been going on of interchange between different cultures, traditions, mythologies. Connections have been falling into place particularly in the realm of mythic symbols, all the more tending to confirm that under all the distinctions we have more in common than otherwise. There is a Golden Thread running through the ages that ties symbols to their perennial referents. "It is amazing, but now undeniable," as Joseph Campbell puts it, "that the vocabulary of symbol is to such an extent constant throughout the world that it must be recognised to represent a single pictorial script, through which

Fig. 32    Two Birds on One Tree,
         Book of Kells, folio 3r

realisations of a *tremendum* experienced through life are given statement. . . Furthermore . . .the signs may be arranged to make fresh poetic statements concerning the great themes of ultimate concern; and from such a pictorial poem new waves of realisation ripple out through the whole range of the world heritage of myth. So that a polymorphic, cross-cultural discourse can be recognised to have been in progress from perhaps the dawn of human culture, opening realisations of the import inherent both in the symbols themselves and in the mysteries of life and thought to which they bring the mind to accord."

This golden thread of symbolic language is what makes the primordial truth intelligible, the unheard audible. Such, as Coomaraswamy tells us, is the task of art, or it is not art.

# Fig. 33   Spiral Branch Construction

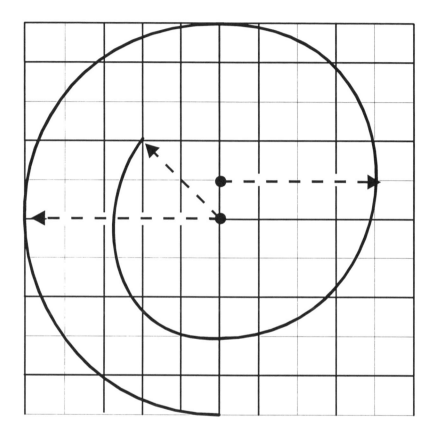

## Fig. 34 Construction of Tree, Muiredach's Cross, Monasterboice

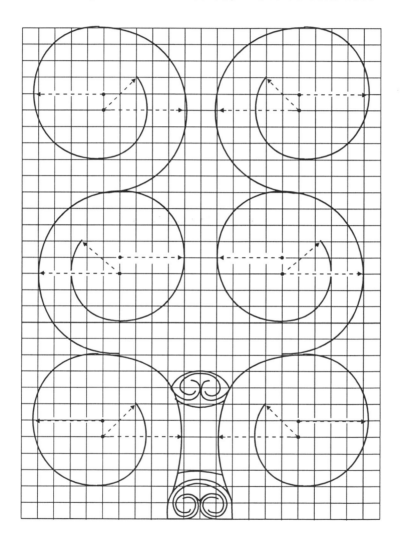

# Fig. 35 Outlined Version, Muiredach's Cross, Monasterboice

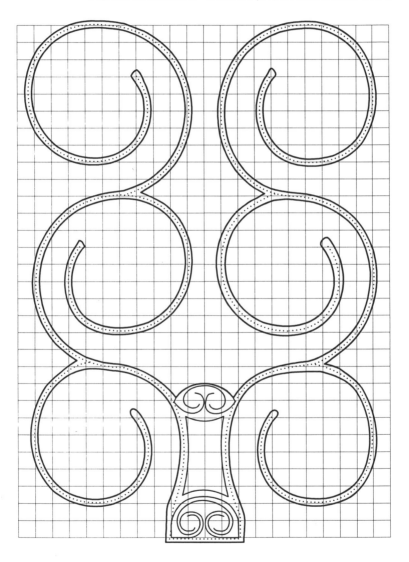

Fig. 36    Lions and Berries Added,
              Muiredach's Cross, Monasterboice

Fig. 37    Lions and Tree Interlaced,
        Muiredach's Cross, Monasterboice

Fig. 38    Birds, Leaves and Ropework Added,
Muiredach's Cross, Monasterboice

# Fig. 39 Completed with Background Filled Muiredach's Cross, Monasterboice

# THE BIRD-FILLED TREE

On the holy boughs of the Celestial Tree
High up in the heavenly fields,
Beyond terrestrial desire
My soul-bird a warm nest has built

                – Hafiz

LTHOUGH TWO BIRDS indeed crown the Tree of Life on Muiredach's Cross, at *fig. 39,* the tree itself is inhabited with lions. We shall explore the Inhabited Tree in a later chapter, but for now we shall see how the motif of the two birds on one tree may be expanded, first into a horizontal border, and then into a rectangular frame, such as on the cover design of this book.

## Fig. 40 The Upside-down Tree, Book of Kells, folio 2r

*Four leaves cause a mistake in the weaving, over-over instead of over-under. Three is better.*

The pot of the tree hangs from the middle of an arch. The upside-down tree is a widespread motif: the Upanishads describe it as Asvattha, "whose roots rise on high and whose branches grow low, it is the pure, the Brahman, what is called Non-Death". The root here is hidden in its pot, as the origin of life is hidden in the womb or vessel of the spirit, which is precisely the import of the medieval term for the vessel, *Vas Spiritualis*. If, as in Celtic gospel books the tree is equated with Christ, then the cup refers to the Virgin as the vessel of the incarnation.

[ 72 ]

## Fig. 41 The Upright Tree

*Here is one solution to the problem, only three leaves woven, the fourth not.*

The shape of the pot is based on two triangles, downward and upward pointing, intersecting at the centre of the vase. When the cup is turned over, of course, upward and downward switch places, illustrating the interplay of opposites. If you held folio 2r of the Book of Kells up to the light, you would see that the base of the pot coincides precisely with the heart of the figure on the reverse of the same sheet, 2v. The layout on the back was traced through from the front, so the placement is deliberate, and significant.

Fig. 42   Two birds, Left Side

The tree is centred, but there are thirteen spirals to the viewer's right and fourteen to the left, odd and even, a further play of opposites, like the sun and moon on the Elamite vase, or Adam and Eve in the garden. But here we have an odd number of birds in an even number of spirals, and *vice versa*, in keeping with the theme of reversal of the tree, and the tendency to the reversal of polarities.

The first spiral on either side of the central and mysterious vessel is empty,

Fig. 43  Two birds, Right Side

leaving twelve birds on the left and thirteen on the right, even number on the
left and odd number on the right.

Even numbers were considered feminine
and odd masculine. The odd-numbered
birds on the right all have their heads
out, the even-numbered to the left have
their heads tucked in, outward going on
the masculine side, inward turning on
the feminine side. The tree therefore is
divided into two sides, and the two sides
are contrasted.

# Fig. 44 Two birds, Left Side

The divided tree is a motif in itself, and very common in Celtic art and legend. It seems to me that this division refers symbolically to the dualistic appearance of life, which seems to be divided into pairs of opposites, through the union of which life propagates itself. On another level, it refers to the fact that each one of us contains two kinds of identity, conditioned and unconditioned, mortal and immortal. The conditioned sort is the

Fig. 45  Two birds, Left Side

personality,  the self-image or ego, that
masks the deeper level, which has no
name or definition, the "true" self. The
conditioned half is the bird that eats the
fruit of the tree.  It ceases at death like a
reflection when the glass breaks. It is
called the *persona*, meaning the mask of
the actor, for it is built up of the role we
choose, or are given to play on the stage
of life; it follows a definite script and
reacts according to the lines it has

Fig. 46   Left Terminal, Book of Kells, folio 2r

learned. It hides the true player, whose real voice is not heard, whose real features are not seen behind the mask.

On the other hand, as the birds on the left side seem to suggest, there is a deeper self behind the mask, within ourselves, the silent witness in us all. These birds seem to be looking within themselves to find it.

The symbol of the divided tree is used a couple of pages later, on folio 4r, as shown at *fig. 48*. There they fill two pillars which support the strange looking creature consisting of the body of the

Fig. 47   Right Terminal, Book of Kells, folio 2r

Lion of St Mark joined to the head of the Calf of St Luke.

As before, the two sides are quite different. The left side has eight spirals, and the right has seven. This corresponds to the left/twelve, right/thirteen of the design on folio 2r. There we had a contrast between the inner and the outer. On folio 4r, however, there are three birds on the left and no birds on the right, a contrast between the manifest and the unmanifest, the plane of accidental circumstance that shapes the soul and the causal plane of pure being, spirit.

Fig. 48   Bird in Tree,
           Book of Kells, folio 4R

a

b

upper half: eight spirals, three birds...

c

These two patterns, figs 48, 49, fill a vertical column, here rotated 90°. The tree
has five-part leaves and some lobed stems.

Fig. 49  The Uninhabited Tree,
Book of Kells, folio 4R

a

*... lower half: seven spirals, no birds*

b

The upper half, fig. 48c, is inhabited by
birds. The lower half, fig. 49b, shows the
same tree without birds or lobed stems.

## Fig. 50  Tree with Three Birds, Book of Kells, folio 4r

a

b

c

## Variations and Permutations

a

b

c

# Fig. 51   Construction of Bird in Tree: 1

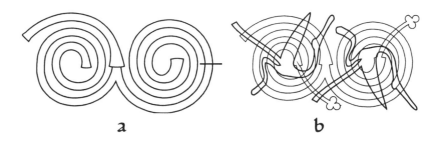

a                              b

a   step one: branches spiral 2 turns from stem
b   step two: add trefoil and bird contour

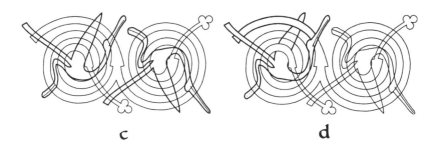

c                              d

Beginning left spiral,
c   step three: divide beak and toes
d   step four: first segment, under tail, over
wing tip

## Fig. 52   Construction of Bird in Tree: 2

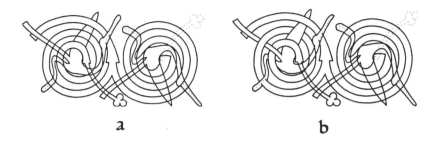

a                                    b

a    step five: under upper jaw, over lower
b    step six: complete weave on wing tail and toes

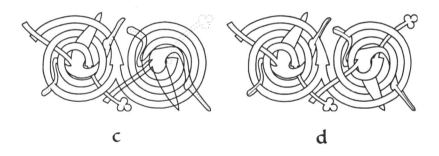

c                                    d

c    step seven: weave neck and trefoil
d    step eight: repeat previous with second bird

## Fig. 53   Grid Construction of Corner: 1

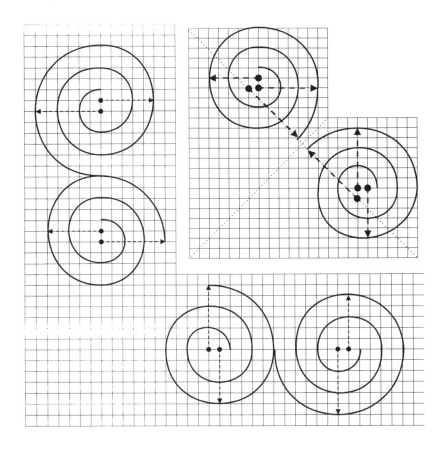

Having designed a repeating unit of the border, the next stage is to construct a corner piece. In this design, the spirals

## Fig. 54   Grid Construction of Corner: 2

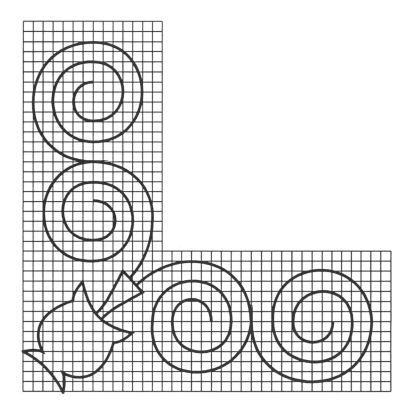

have to be positioned so that they come together in the corner, where they converge in the main stem.

# Fig. 55   Grid Construction of Corner: 3

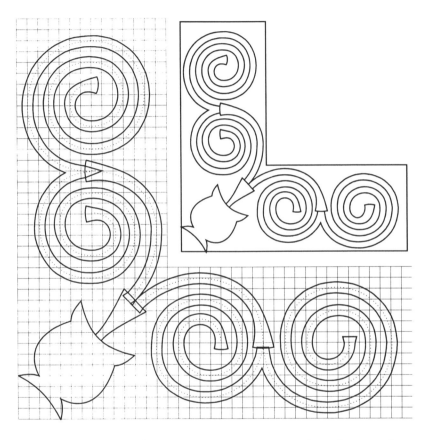

Now outline the spiral lines to the desired
width of the branches. It may be thicker
or thinner than as shown here.

## Fig. 56   Grid Construction of Corner: 4

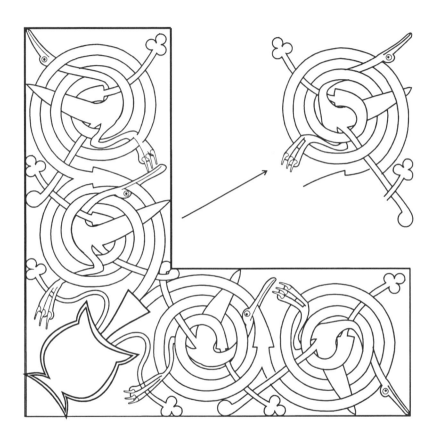

Apply steps as shown in figs 51,52 to weave birds and tree. On the upright arm, the weaving is reversed (compare inset).

# Fig. 57 Grid Construction of corner: 5

Having woven the two arms of the mitred corner piece so that the weaving is reversed - where a section passes over another in the horizontal arm, it passes under at the corresponding place in the other arm - the corner unit may be rotated $90°$ so that the two end units that come together along the bottom edge of the border will be woven in reverse relative to one another, rather than if they were just mirrored, as in the inset.

This allows the necks of the birds or the stems of the trefoils to be woven properly when the two corners are joined along the bottom edge.

Rotated four times, a corner may be used to create a simple square frame, fig. 58.

## Fig. 58   Square Frame, Discontinuous

Having turned the
corner bracket 90°,
it can then be extended
one unit along the
upright arm,
as shown at
figs 59, 60.

# Fig. 59  Lower Left-hand Corner Layout

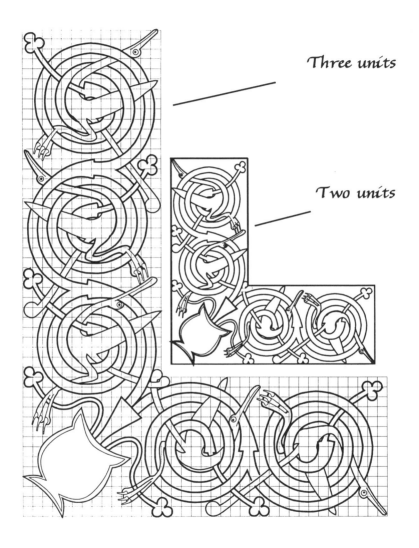

Three units

Two units

## Fig. 60   Lower Right-hand Corner Layout

Three units

Two units

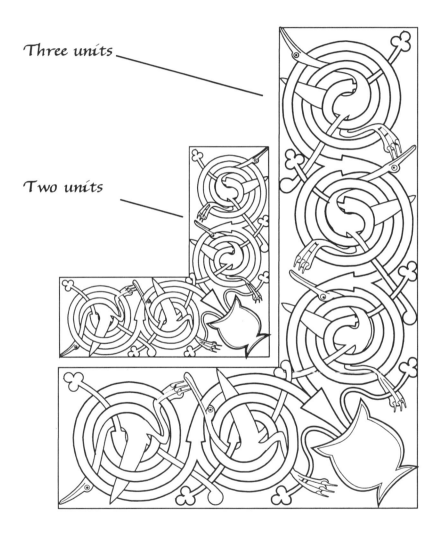

# Fig. 61   Lower Left-hand Corner

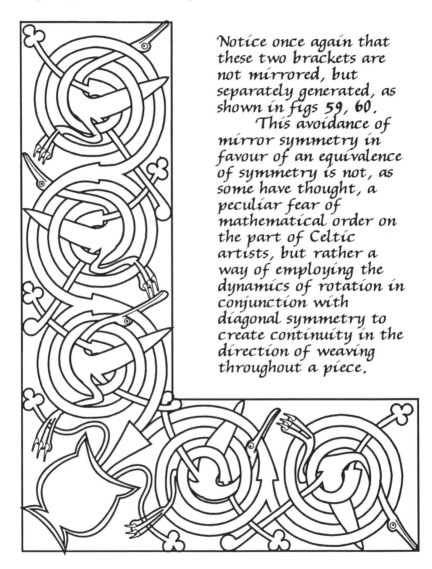

Notice once again that these two brackets are not mirrored, but separately generated, as shown in figs **59, 60**.

This avoidance of mirror symmetry in favour of an equivalence of symmetry is not, as some have thought, a peculiar fear of mathematical order on the part of Celtic artists, but rather a way of employing the dynamics of rotation in conjunction with diagonal symmetry to create continuity in the direction of weaving throughout a piece.

## Fig. 62   Lower Right-hand Corner

The idea here is to achieve a reversal of the weave between corresponding units at the mid-point of each side.

This will allow a joining of the units into one continuous border, in which the direction of the weaving will be maintained, and which will also create a diagonal symmetry, as illustrated in figs 63,64.

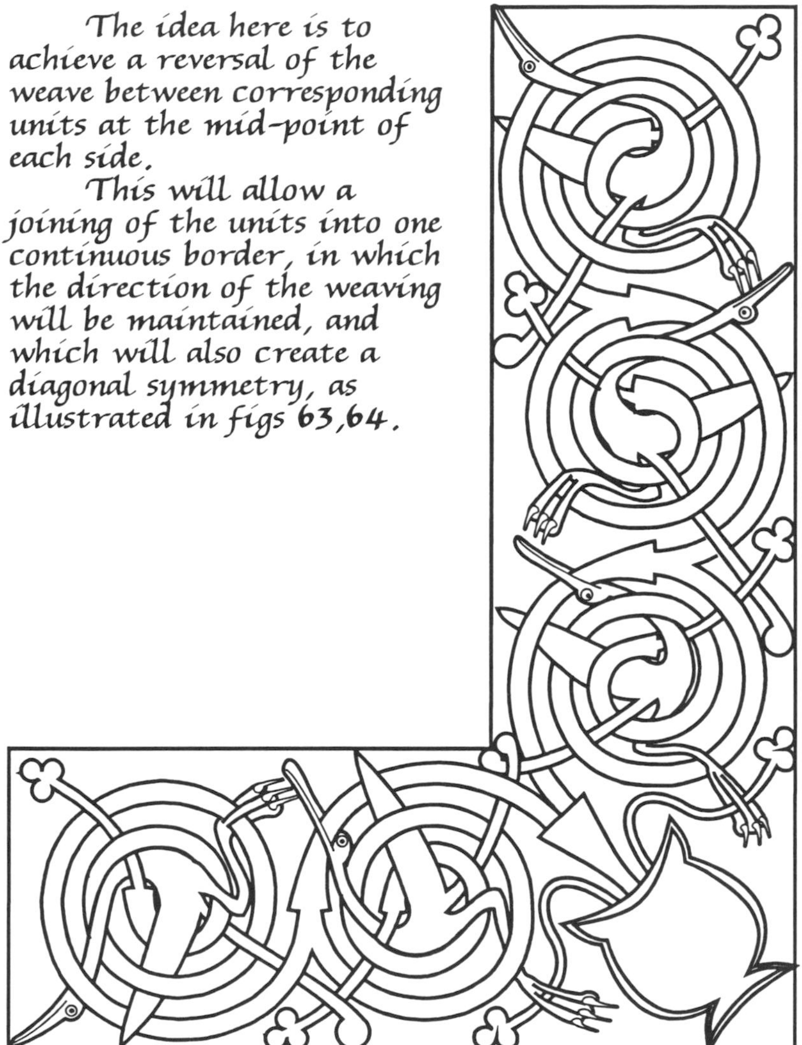

## Fig. 63   Frame of Four Corner Units

## Fig. 64  The Continuous Border

Fig. 65  Book of Kells, Detail from
Border, Chi-Rho Page

# CHE INHABICED CREE

*I have a hut in the wood,*
*none knows it but my Lord;*
*an ash tree this side, a hazel on the other,*
*a great tree on a mound encloses it*

—ANON, IRISH, 10TH CENTURY

 HE FOUR – LEGGED ANIMAL
that appears in the Tree of Life
in the Book of Kells is not
the dog of Northumbrian
manuscripts such as the Book
of Lindisfarne, but the Lion, whose
association with the tree goes back to the
Winged Lion of the earliest traditions in
the Middle East, as we have seen in the
first chapter.

# Fig. 66 Lion in Tree,
## Book of Kells, folio 258r

a    Pencilled layout

b    The same, woven

c    The unit filled, and flipped horizontally.

The lion is not always shown with a mane, particularly in instances such as this where the original is drawn on a minute scale. But the characteristic feature which conventionally distinguishes the feline from the canine is the length of the snout, the cat's being a snubbed nose drawn with a definite spiral as here, *fig. 66.*

*This example is based on a corner unit of a frame, mitred at 45°, like a wooden picture frame. I have flipped it here to make a length mitred at each end.*

Fig. 67 Inhabited Tree Border,
Book of Kells, folio 285R

a

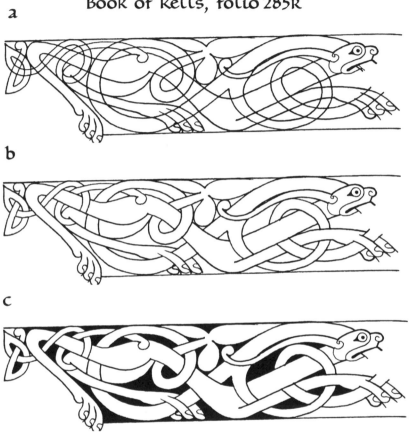

b

c

This is the lower left-hand corner unit
on the left side of a border, which I have
rotated to read horizontally.

Fig. 68  Inhabited Tree Border,
Book of Kells, folio 285R

a

b

c

On the left is the head of the animal from
the previous figure, showing the overlap
with the rear end of a second animal.

Fig. 69 Inhabited Tree Border,
Book of Kells, folio 285R

a

b

c

On the left, the front end of the lion of
the previous figure overlapping the rear-
end of the third lion whose head appears

Fig. 70    Inhabited Tree Border,
a        Book of Kells, folio 285R

b

c

at the left of *fig. 70*. The fourth lion's paw
touches the pot of the Tree of Life,  mid-
way through the pattern.

Fig. 71    Inhabited Tree Border,
           Book of Kells, folio 285 r

a

b

c

The first lion to the right of the pot
touches paws with the second, whose
head is shown on the right.

Fig. 72   Inhabited Tree Border,
Book of Kells, folio 285R

a

b

c

The second lion, shown here from the
neck down, touches the paw of the third
lion.

Fig. 73   Inhabiτeδ Tree BoRδeR,
Book of Kells, folio 285 R

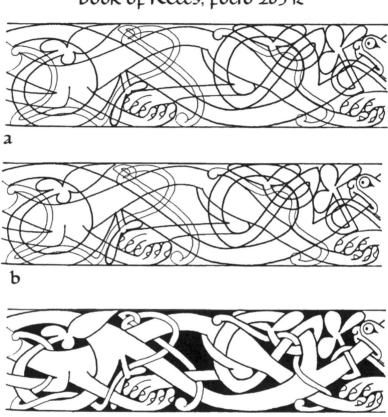

a

b

c

The third lion's body is on the left, the
fourth lion's head is on the right. The
fourth lion's ear ends in a leaf shape.

Fig. 74 Inhabited Tree Border,
Book of Kells, folio 285 r

a

b

c

The fourth lion's hind leg and tail fill the
45° mitre of the corner. This unit com-
pletes one side of the frame.

---

Fig. 75   Inhabited Tree, Kells, Layout

   You will recognise this as the illuminated panel from the *In Principio* page
of St John's Gospel in the Book of Kells,
that we studied in *fig. 1*, which is really
an Inhabited Tree. As I was doing it, I
noticed that there were about a dozen
mistakes in the weaving. I corrected them
as I went along, *fig. 76*. In the spirit of
the game, "Spot the Deliberate Mistakes",
you may like to see how many you can

## Fig. 76    Inhabited Tree, Book of Kells

find. If you first lightly trace the layout from an enlarged copy of *fig.* 75, with a hard lead pencil, then weave it with a softer pencil before inking it up, the changes I have made will become apparent while comparing *figs* I and 76.

On the following pages, I have extracted the letters, and as they depend on the tree for interlacement, I have given alternative constructions for the knots.

# Fig. 77 Letters R,1

## Fig. 78 Letter N

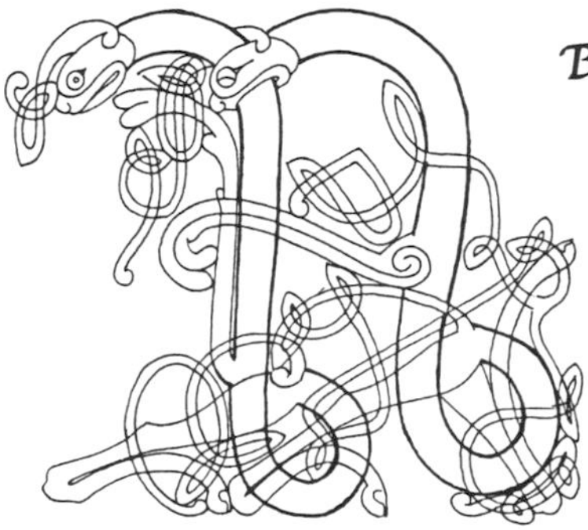

Left: the original layouts.
Below: suggested arrangements
for the knots.
Filled versions of the three
letters below are shown
above at fig. 4. You can
colour in the ones here in
the same manner, with
black or another colour
such as red, for in-
stance. The letters
at fig. 77 may be
given a thin line
as here, in
brown ink, for
instance.

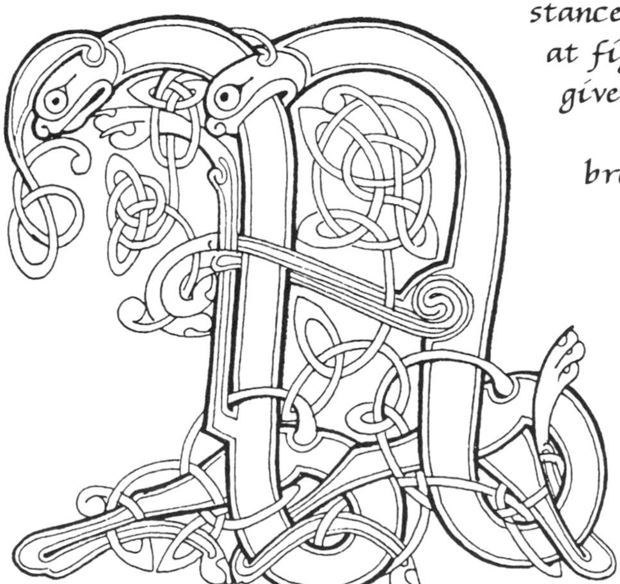

## Fig. 79   Lions / Letters in the Tree of Life

This panel of illuminated letters consists of lions in the tree. They form the letters ACHA, part of the name Zacharias. They belong to the Lion Alphabet from the Book of Kells which I published in an earlier book in this series, Illuminated Letters.

# TREE AND LEAF

*Blessed is the man who has found wisdom...*
*Her ways are good ways, and all her paths are peaceful,*
*She is a tree of life to all that lay hold upon her.*

—PROVERBS 3: 18

 TAKE THE TREE WITHOUT animals or birds in it to be a reference to the branch. Early Christians knew that the word Nazerene meant "the Branch", as Zachariah had prophecied: "I will bring forth my servant the BRANCH" (Zachariah 3:8), and, "Behold the man whose name is The Branch; and he shall grow up out of his place, and he shall build the temple of the Lord" (Zachariah 6:12).

# Fig. 80   Tree From North Cross, Dulleek, Ireland

This figure combines spiral, knot and tree forms, stemming from the triquetra knot, in place of the pot, perhaps alluding to the Trinity. Crawford sees this as a "representation of the vine which differs from the usual type, in being without the birds and animals often placed amongst the branches. In this design the tree has been reduced to an abstract pattern; the branching form and bunches of grapes alone indicating the vine."

## Fig. 81  Border  Adaptation
### Based on the Previous Figure

## Fig. 82 From Book of Kells, folio 32v

This flowering tree with trefoil leaves forms a heart rising out of a pot which is based on the saltire or diagonal cross, synonymous with the Greek letter X, or Chi, the initial of the name of Christ. The form of the flower is based on the geometry of the hexagon, six circles surrounding a seventh at the centre.

Fig. 83    Triquetra Tree Panel, Kells,

Construction of tree  shown on following pages,
figs. 85-90.

I once heard the analogy of the two birds on one tree used to refer to the two hemispheres of the brain, with the spine as the tree. The interpretation extends to the pot, in that it implies the portability of the plant, it can move around, and is not rooted in one spot.

I mention it in passing, by way of introducing the following section in which I present some geometrical studies of the construction of the tree from the Book of Kells, *fig. 83*.

Some people, the right-brained, find it easy to read drawings, to see the lines, and imagine it being drawn as they look, so that they can then put pen to paper and replicate the process as they have visualised it. Such people sometimes find grids annoying because they do not need them. Others find drawing daunting, and prefer the grid approach, which helps them to see the whole design in the mind's eye, after which drawing it is easier.

Fig. 84   Geometry of Tendril

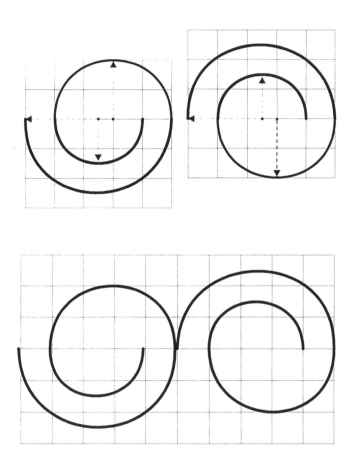

# Fig. 85   Geometry of Tree: 1

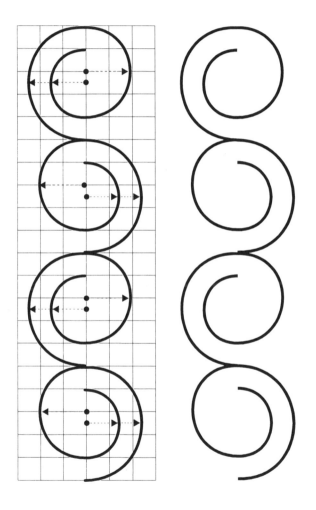

# Fig. 86　Geometry of Tree: 2

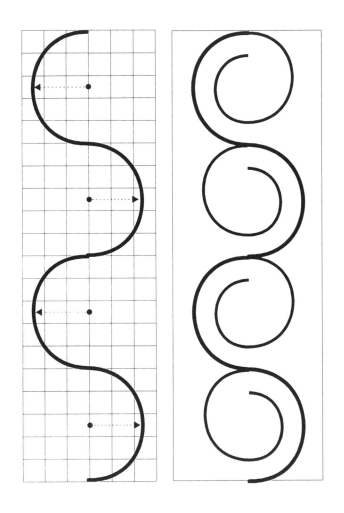

# Fig. 87   Grid Construction: 1

# Fig. 88  Grid Construction: 2

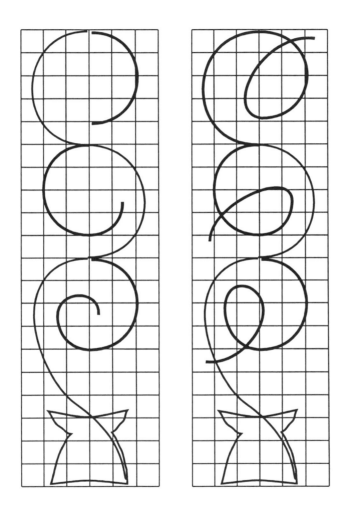

# Fig. 89 Key-stroke Construction: 1

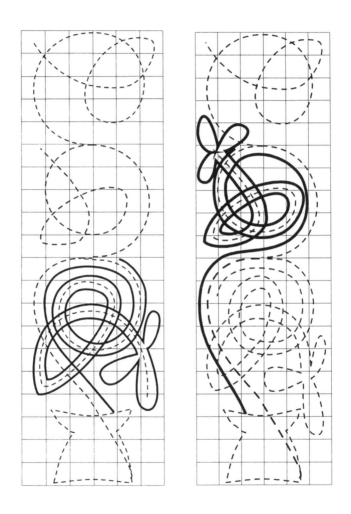

Fig. 90   Pencilled Layout;   Final Draft

Figs 91-96 show twelve stages of construction of the tree, in which the main
lines of the tendril may be laid out with
a pair of compasses, figs 91-94, pencilled
up, woven and finally inked, figs. 95-96.

A word about grids in general. There
have been arguments about whether grids
are relevant to Celtic art or not. The
view against has been articulated by Liam
de Paor.

"The order comes from within: this is
the key to what is 'Celtic' in Irish art of
the early Christian period. It cannot be
imposed by a T-Square and set-square, or
marked off by numbers like the lay-out
of a Roman camp, nor even guided by a
development of harmonic modules like a
Greek tablature: it spirals out from the
heart of the design; it expresses neither
essence nor being but constant becoming,
and the artist must have been as fully
engaged in every veering of a line as in
the planning of his overall design. . . The

master calligrapher can charge and poise
his brush, stare at and absorb the blank
page, and then swiftly place the right
shape in the right balance in the right
place. . . This is why modern imitations
of 'Celtic' (i. e. early Irish) manuscript
pages, which depend on elaborate, imposed, setting-out patterns of squares,
rectangles, triangles and compass-drawn
curves, are as dead as doornails"

In fact, the old manuscripts were
meticulously laid out before hand, de-
pending precisely on setting out patterns
of squares and compass-drawn curves.
Much of what is bad about poor Celtic
art today is that it follows Liam de Paor's
advice. What he says may apply to Zen
calligraphy, but not to the western
scribe, who needs to rule the page and
have absolute command over proportions
and angles. *Art without Science is nothing*,
was the philosophy of the medieval scribes,
as well as of true artists of all periods.

Fig. 91 The Construction of the Tree, Step 1; Step 2

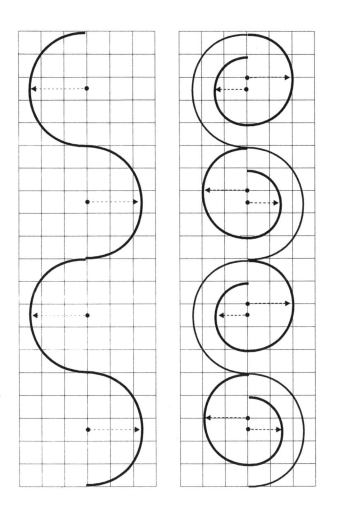

Fig. 92   The Construction of the Tree
Step 3;   Step 4

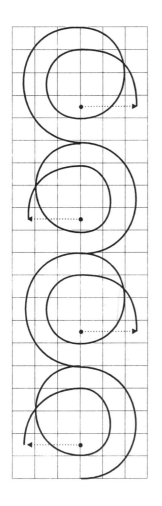
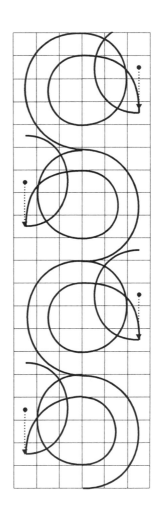

Fig. 93 The Construction of the Tree, Step 5; Step 6

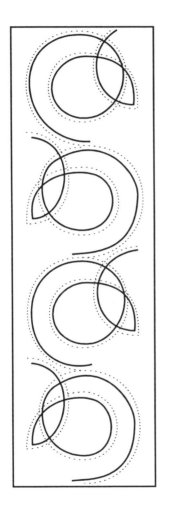 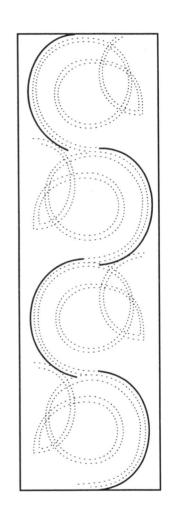

Fig. 94   The Construction of the Tree,
           Step 7; Step 8

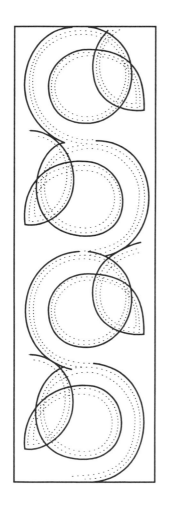
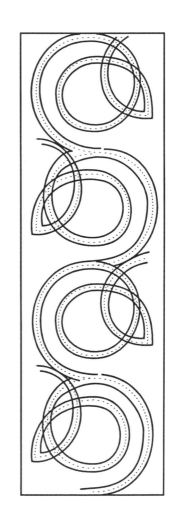

Fig. 95   The Construction of the Tree
Step 9; Step 10

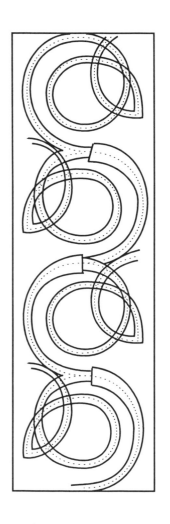 

Fig. 96    The Construction of the Tree
            Step 11; Step 12

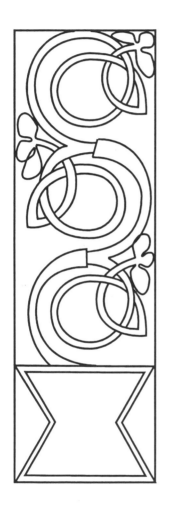

Of the kind of art we find in the Book
of Kells, Liam de Paor concluded that "it
repels and fascinates because its order,
barely controlling an explosive anarchy,
allows us to glimpse the chaos at the
heart of the universe which our own
Romanised culture is at pains to con-
ceal." Rather, order is central to the art.

The order which is evident on every
page of the Book of Kells stems from the
traditional world-view of the time: in
the language of cosmogony, the beginning
and end of any plane of existence is defined by its centre. Every phenomenon
emerges on to or is born into a particular
plane of existence, expands from that point
to the limit of its being and contracts
towards a point of departure from that
plane. At the point of ultimate contraction
it ceases to exist on that plane and is trans-
formed into another mode or dimension
of existence. On any plane, the point of
emergence and the point of ultimate re-

turn are both incorporated in the symbol of the centre. The cyclical round of existence is symbolised as the circumference of the circle. The symbol of the centre, par excellence, is the cross. The mathematical centre is defined by the intersection of the horizontal by the vertical dimension. The dimensions were traditionally interpreted as relating to consciousness: the vertical corresponding to the axial pole of the unconditioned Principle of Identity, while the horizontal corresponding to the plane on which that identity takes on form. The plane symbolises the world of phenomena that condition the existence of a being. The vertical dimension of identity, however, is not so conditioned, it remains apart from the plane of the circle intersecting it, giving rise to its conditions and controlling their limits from the centre. Clearly, geometry is essential to this traditional view.

Fig. 97    Spiral Stem and Trefoil
           Anti-clockwise Unit: Step 1

a

b

Figs 97-106 show how to weave the spiral stem and the trefoil, stroke by stroke. This is a simple exercise for beginners, and good practice for the experienced who would like to improve their line-work. Unless you are Giotto, who could draw a perfect circle free hand, you will need to lay out the spiral geometrically, at least once. Then you can trace it over on each side of the sheet, transferring the imprint of the centre line, as in *figs 97a, 101a*.

Begin with the transferred pencil line of the spiral and trileaf, which can be drawn with a single stroke without lifting the pencil, *fig. 97a*. With practice, you should be able to draw the spiral and the leaf together, having repeatedly imitated the geometrical model until it has been learned off by heart, as you would learn a piece of music from a score, before performing it without having to look at the music. Practice alone makes perfect.

The next step is to outline the centre
line, *fig. 98 a.* The spiral has become a
triline – itself a symbol of the union of
opposites – with the centreline the third,
synthesizing factor that mediates between
polarities, which controls them. It will
be erased later, but it is always there
implicitly, in every band, ribbon, or
path. It symbolises the centre in motion,
radiating and expanding out from the
centre of the triquetra line of the trefoil.
Symbolically, any spiral begins at the
centre and moves outward, as does the
universe. This is its real direction.

The outline of the leaf, of course is
not doubled, simply follow its contour.
The outlining can also be done in a single
stroke, without lifting the pencil from
beginning to end, with practice. Then
you may impress everyone with your
calligraphic mastery, but remember:
stare first at the paper, poise, then place
it just so. It looks more artistic.

Fig. 98    Spiral Stem and Trefoil
Anti-clockwise Unit: Step 2

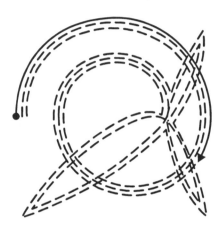

a

Lay the first segment with slightly heavier
pencil, as at b.

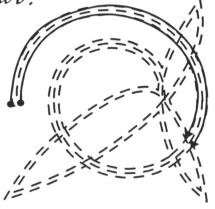

b

## Fig. 99    Spiral Stem and Trefoil
## Anti-clockwise Unit: Steps 3, 4

*Lay second leaf, a, then second segment, b.*

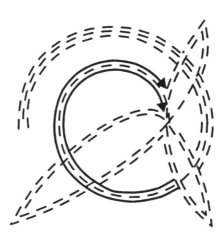

a

b

Fig. 100   Spiral Stem and Trefoil
           Anti-clockwise Unit: Steps 5, 6

Lay first leaf and third leaf under stem
segments, a.

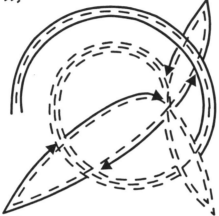

a

Ink up, and erase pencil to complete, b.

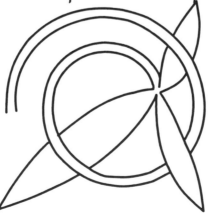

b

# Fig. 101 Spiral Stem and Trefoil Clockwise Unit: Step 1

Pencil spiral and trefoil in single stroke, a.

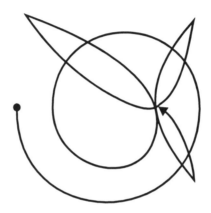

a

Pencil outline with single stroke, b.

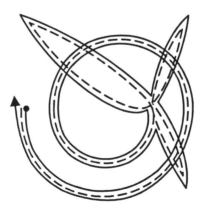

b

Fig. 102   Spiral Stem and Trefoil
            Clockwise Unit: Step 2

Pencilled triline, a.

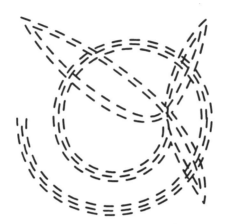

a

Trace over first segment, b.

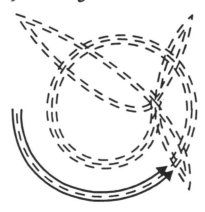

b

## Fig. 103    Spiral Stem and Trefoil Clockwise Unit: Step 3

Pencil over first leaf, a.

a

Pencil over second segment, b.

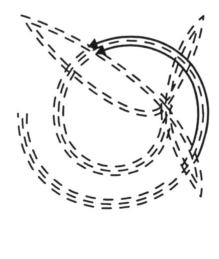

b

## Fig. 104  Spiral Stem and Trefoil
## Clockwise Unit: Step 4

Pencil second leaf under segment two, a.

a

Pencil third leaf, b.

b

## Fig. 105  Spiral Stem and Trefoil Clockwise Unit: Step 5

Pencil over last segment, a.

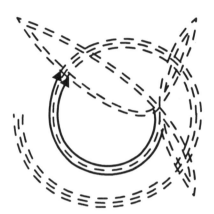

a

Ink up, b.

b

Fig. 106  Spiral Stem and Trefoil
Clockwise Unit: Step 6

Erase centre line, a.

a

The leaves may be decorated, b.

b

# Fig. 107    Tree Border, Kells, 8r

a    Freehand        b    Geometrical Layout

Fig. 108      Tile Repeat

Three units from previous figure.

Fig. 109   Tree of Life, Book of Kells,
Left-hand Side, folio 8r

The right side spirals all have four-
leafed centres or quatrefoils; the left side
has three quatrefoil spirals and two trefoil spirals.  The even-numbered leaf does
not weave properly in seven cases, except
for the two units on either side of the
pot. The artist has tried it several ways,
and finally reverted to three-leafed centres at the far left of the border, which
does work.

Fig. 110　Tree of Life, Book of Kells,
　　　　　Right-hand Side, folio 8r

Another possible way to use the even
numbered leaf without causing a weaving
problem is to add an extra stem with
berries on the end, sprouting from between the leaves, as at *fig. III*. The form is
similar to the leaf and spiral exercise
with three leaves, *figs 97-106*, where the
stem of the berries replaces the central
leaf. The exercise at *fig. III* may be used
with two leaves and berries, or with four
leaves and berries.

# Fig. 111 Tree of Life, Leaf and Berry

a

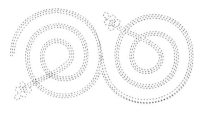

a  trace centreline and outline in pencil

b  alternate weaving so that one unit is the reverse of the other

c  repeat units in reverse weave

b

d  reflect opposite halves, to form fork at centre of tree, maintaining weaving order, add pot to centre.

The final stages are shown at fig. 112 a,b, c.

c

d

Fig. 112    Tree of Life, Leaf and Berry

a

b

c

# Fig. 113  Border, Anglian Cross-Shaft, Kirk of Morham, East Lothian

This design is taken from an Anglian Cross shaft of c. AD 750– 850, and shows a certain affinity with the Celtic Tree of Life, particularly in the use of berries and the swelling of the stems like trumpets at the forks. The narrow centreline is used instead of a centre band, and is an effect used a lot by the Vikings. The split leaf at *fig. 114* is also like later Viking art, but we find it in the Book of Kells also. Unlike the Book of Kells, however, here we have leaves shown in profile rather than

Fig. 114   Border, Anglian Cross-Shaft,
Kirk of Morham, East Lothian

full face, and the tendrils do not spiral
completely.

In the next figure, I have shown what
this figure might look like if it were de-
veloped as a Tree of Life border with the
motif reflected, and a pot added. There is
enough variety in the original to generate
a pair of matching panels, *fig. 115*. While
very similar in form, I think that in these
Anglian designs we have more of a medieval than a Celtic style of Tree of Life.

Fig. 115    Variations on Anglian Cross-
Shaft Border, Kirk of Morham,

# RECOMMENDED BOOKS

George Bain, *Celtic Art*, Glasgow, 1951

Joseph Campbell, *The Masks of God: Occidental Mythology*, New York, 1964

Joseph Campbell, Charles Musees, *In All Her Names*, San Francisco, 1991

Tom Chetwynd, *A Dictionary of Symbols*, London, 1982

Roger Cook, *The Tree of Life*, London, 1974

Ananda Coomaraswamy, *Figures of Speech or Figures of Thought*, London, 1947

Henry S. Crawford, *Irish Carved Ornament*, Cork, 1980

James G. Frazer, *The Golden Bough: A Study in Comparative Religion*, London, 1890

Françoise Henry, *Irish High Crosses*, Dublin, 1964

*Irish Art*, Volume 2, London, 1970

*The Book of Kells*, London, 1974

James Joyce, *Portrait of the Artist as a Young Man*, New York, 1956

Aidan Meehan, *Celtic Design: A Beginner's Manual*, London, 1991

*Celtic Design: Knotwork, The Secret Method of the Scribes*, London, 1991

*Celtic Design: Animal Patterns*, London, 1992

*Celtic Design: Illuminated Letters*, London, 1992

*Celtic Design: Spiral Patterns*, London, 1993

*Celtic Design: Maze Patterns*, London, 1993

*Celtic Design: The Dragon and the Griffin, The Viking Impact*, London, 1995

Carl Nordenfalk, *Celtic and Anglo-Saxon Painting*, London, 1977

James Powell, *The Tao of Symbols*, New York, 1982

Anne Ross, *Pagan Celtic Britain*, London, 1967

Hilary Richardson, John Scarry, *An Introduction to Irish High Crosses*, Dublin, 1990

G. M. Trevelyan, *The Mingling of the Races*, London, 1934